Slurp Burp!

Jane Langford
Illustrated by Barbara Vagnozzi

It was spring.
Baby Bear was asleep in the den.

"Come on," said Mum. "Wake up.
It is time to go outside."

3

Mum took two big steps.
Baby Bear took ten little steps.
"Look out!" said Mum. "Icicles!"

Jingle! Jangle!

4

"Too late!" said Baby Bear.

Mum took two big steps.
Baby Bear took ten little steps.
They came to the top of a hill.
"Let's slide!" said Mum.

Whoosh

"Mind the bump!" said Mum.

8

"Too late!" said Baby Bear.

Ouch!

9

10

They found some water.
"Let's drink," said Mum.

Crack!

"Mind the ice!" said Mum.

splash!

"Too late!" said Baby Bear.

They found some fish.
"Let's eat!" said Mum.

"Too late!" said Baby Bear.